POETS BE

MW01029116

Library of Congress Catalog Card Number: 83-71474
ISBN 0-910043-05-1

Text copyright 1983 by Jiro Nakano, M.D. and Kay Nakano
Illustrations copyright 1983 by George Hoshida
All rights reserved. This book, or parts thereof, may not be reproduced in
any form without permission. Printed in the United States.

Some of the poems in this book have appeared in *Bamboo Ridge, The
Hawaii Writers' Quarterly*, No. 15, June 1982, Bamboo Ridge Press and in
The Hawaii Herald, April 16 through June 4, 1982, Vol. 3, No. 8, 9, 10 and
11, Hawaii Hochi, Ltd.

Published by Bamboo Ridge Press and the Hawaii Ethnic Resources Center: Talk Story, Inc.

Project Coordinators: Marie Hara and Arnold Hiura

This project is supported by a grant from the National Endowment for the
Arts in Washington, D.C., a federal agency. It is also supported, in part,
by a grant from the State Foundation on Culture and the Arts (SFCA).
The SFCA is funded by grants from the Hawaii State Legislature and by
grants from the National Endowment for the Arts.

Bamboo Ridge Press
P.O. Box 61781
Honolulu, Hawaii 96839-1781
(808) 599-4823

10 9 8 7 6 5 4 3   91 92 93 94 95

POETS BEHIND BARBED WIRE

Tanka Poems

Keiho Soga Taisanboku Mori Sojin Takei Muin Ozaki

Illustrations by George Hoshida

Edited and Translated by Jiro Nakano and Kay Nakano

Acknowledgments

We are deeply grateful to Mr. Muin Ozaki, Mr. Sojin Takei, Dr. Victor M. Mori, the son of the late Taisanboku Mori, and Mrs. Miya Soga, the daughter-in-law of the late Keiho Soga, for their kindness in giving us permission to translate the tanka poems written by the four poets. In the preparation of the anthology, we are particularly indebted to Frances Kakugawa, Yuriko Higa, Esta Cabral, Margaret Kuwada and Philip Miyamoto for reading the manuscript. We also wish to acknowledge John D. Griffith, editor of *Kani Lehua,* Eric Chock and Darrell H.Y. Lum, Co-editors of *Bamboo Ridge,* and Kenneth H. Toguchi of the *Hawaii Herald* for personally publishing selections from the anthology. And to Arnold T. Hiura of the Hawaii Ethnic Resources Center: Talk Story, Inc. for coordinating the publication of this anthology.

Printed and designed by Elepaio Press
Second Printing, 1984

CONTENTS

INTRODUCTION

This anthology of tanka poems, translated from the Japanese into English, seeks to present the story of the Japanese internees in our Wartime Relocation Camps, who, under adverse conditions, created one of the most remarkable examples of emotional and spiritual expression in the history of human arts.

It has been more than 40 years since 110,000 people of Japanese ancestry, including 70,000 American-born citizens, were forcefully removed from their homes and working places to be incarcerated in detention camps without trial. Since early 1981, the Commission on Wartime Relocation and Internment of Civilians, created by Congress in 1980, has held a series of hearings at which many Japanese-Americans attested to the injustice, abuse and mistreatment of innocent people by the United States Government during World War II. Very few people, however, are aware that many of the Japanese internees recorded their life behind barbed wire through Japanese poetic forms such as haiku and tanka. In view of the scarcity of writing paper, these short poems, being less cumbersome than long diaries, were ideal forms for the internees' expression of their pent-up emotions. It also perpetuates the Japanese tradition of expressing their innermost emotions through short poems instead of prose.

For the past few years, we have been researching old tanka poems written by the Issei and Japanese-Americans before and during World War II. In the process we have come across many poems which were written at the concentration camps and which were included in camp magazines and later published in anthologies and Japanese newspapers in Hawaii. Although expressed in just a few lines, each of these tanka is in many respects more explicit and poignant in revealing humiliation, agony, loneliness and despair than the thousands of words spoken at the recent Congressional hearings. We realize that the translation of any poem may lose some of its poetic beauty, nuances and emotional intensity; we have done our utmost, however, to give more readers a better understanding and appreciation for the feeling of these people who were forced to live within barbed wire enclosed camps.

For those who are not familiar with tanka, it is the second shortest poetic form in the world, next to haiku, and consists of 31 syllables (5-7-5-7-7). It originated in fifth century Japan and is still popular today. Tanka speaks of nature as well as human emotions and allows the reader to perceive the unsaid and the intimated.

THE POETS

Keiho Yasutaro Soga (1873-1957)

Born on March 19, 1873 and graduated from Tokyo Hogakuin (Tokyo Law College), Yasutaro Soga came to Hawaii on March 5, 1896. After working as a salesman for stores in Waianae and Waipahu, Oahu, he moved to Kaunakakai, Molokai for two years, where he toiled in heavy labor with other Japanese immigrants on the sugar plantation and experienced much hardship and discrimination.

In 1899, he was hired as editor of the *Hawaii Shimpo,* a Japanese language newspaper in Honolulu which was run by Chuzaburo Shiozawa. Seven years later, he became editor-in-chief of the Japanese language newspaper, the *Yamamoto Shimbun,* and changed its name to the *Nippu Jiji* (Nippon Hawaii Times). Later he became the owner and president of the newspaper. Soga, who devoted 57 years to the Japanese language newspaper, was called "the father of Hawaii Japanese newspaper" and was regarded as the most influential voice in the Japanese community in Hawaii during his days.

In 1911, when the first Oahu plantation labor strike occurred, he sympathized with the Japanese laborers, and spoke against the injustices and discriminatory labor practices of the management. Because of his strong stand against the established business community in Hawaii, he was imprisoned for two years. His courage and leadership, however, received much respect and admiration from the Japanese immigrants.

In 1924, he toured Korea, Manchuria and China, and wrote a travel report, "Sen-Man-Shi No Hatsutabi — Nira No Nioi" (My First Trip to Korea-Manchuria-China — Smell of Chives) which was well received. Thereafter, he visited Japan and China on several occasions, and wrote another travel report, "Nichi-Man O Nozoku" (My Visit to Japan and China).

Among his many cultural interests and hobbies were Yokyoku recitation, Go-Shogi (Japanese chess games), and tanka poems. In

1

1922, Soga, along with Dr. Taisanboku Mori and 15 other Japanese poets, founded the first tanka club in Hawaii called "Choon-shisha" (The Sound of the Sea Tanka Club). Out of the several thousand tanka which he composed during his lifetime, 854 poems were selected and compiled by his former club members, Kempu Kawazoe, Muin Ozaki, Suikei Furuya, Nobuji Yoshida and Sojin Takei, into an anthology, *Keiho Kashu.*

When the war broke out on December 7, 1941, he was immediately arrested by the FBI, and incarcerated first at Sand Island Military Camp and later shipped to Angel Island Prison in California. Thereafter, he was interned at Lordsburg, New Mexico and Santa Fe Relocation Camp where he founded the Santa Fe-shisha Tanka Club with the tanka poets from Hawaii and California. He remained at the Santa Fe Camp until the end of the war, and returned to Honolulu on November 13, 1945.

Upon his return to Honolulu, he changed the name of *Nippu Jiji* to *Hawaii Times* and yielded the presidency to his son, Shigeo, but continued to write editorials and columns. Also in 1946, he reactivated the Choon-shisha along with others. In 1948, he wrote a documentary book on the internment of the Japanese-Americans during the war, called *Tessaku Seikatsu* (Life Behind the Barbed Wire Fence). His monumental work, *Goiyunenkan No Hawaii Kaiko* (My Hawaii Memoirs of 50 Years) and *Hawaii Sono Oriori* (Life in Hawaii) were published in 1953. As an active member of the Makiki Christian Church, his devotion and contributions were immeasurable. He died on March 3, 1957.

Keiho Soga's poems were selected from his tanka anthology, *Keiho Kashu* (Collection of Tanka Poems by Keiho) containing 854 tanka poems, published by his wife, Mrs. Seiko Soga, October 25, 1957, Honolulu.

Taisanboku Motokazu Mori (1890-1958)

Dr. Motokazu Mori, who was born in Nagasaki, Japan on July 24, 1890, was the son of the most noted pioneer physician to Hawaii, Dr. Iga Mori (1864-1951). After receiving his M.D. degree in 1916 from the Kyushu Imperial University in Fukuoka, Japan, he came to Hawaii in 1918 and went to the Mayo Clinic for further medical study. He returned to Honolulu in 1920 to practice medicine in association with his father. In 1936, he was awarded a Ph.D from the Tokyo Imperial University. His dissertation was on climatically changed blood composition of second generation Japanese-Americans.

In 1921, he married Miss Misao Harada, daughter of Dr. Tasuke Harada, Professor of Oriental Language at the University of Hawaii, and eventually had three boys and one girl. After his wife died in 1927, he married Dr. Ishiko Shibuya who was a physician at Kuakini Hospital, Honolulu.

As one of the founders of the Choon-shisha, he was active in the literary circle in Honolulu, and composed thousands of tanka poems under the pen name, Taisanboku. His second wife also joined the Choon-shisha with Shakunage as her pen name. She was a part-time news correspondent for *The Japan Times* in Tokyo.

When the war broke out, both Dr. Mori and his wife, Ishiko, were arrested by the FBI and incarcerated in separate quarters of the military camp on Sand Island, Honolulu. On September 16, 1942, he was sent to Angel Island, California aboard a military transport. From there, he was transferred to the Santa Fe Relocation Camp in New Mexico and then to the Crystal City Internment Camp in Texas where he was finally united with his wife. During their sojourn in Crystal City, Motokazu and Ishiko Mori founded a tanka poetry club called "Texas-shisha" with Sojin Takei, and held regular meetings of the internee tanka poets. Toward the end of the war, Mori and Takei compiled an anthology, *Nagareboshi* (Shooting Star), of the tanka poems written by the members, and published it in mimeographed form shortly before departure from Crystal City. He returned to Honolulu on December 7, 1945.

After his return he opened his medical practice and also helped reactivate the Choon-shisha. He died in Honolulu on January 21, 1958. He was not only a leader in the medical society, but also a prominent figure in the Japanese community and the literary circle in Honolulu.

Taisanboku Mori's poems were selected from the Texas-shisha tanka anthology, *Nagareboshi,* containing 334 tanka poems by 31 internees, published on October 22, 1945 shortly before his departure from Crystal City, Texas.

Sojin Tokiji Takei (1903-   )

Tokiji Takei was born in Asakura-mura, Fukuoka-ken, Japan, on April 6, 1903 and came to Maui to join his parents in 1922 soon after graduating from a high school in Fukuoka. Two years later, in 1924, he became a Japanese language school teacher in Kahului, Maui. From 1930, he taught at the Paia Japanese language school until 1933 when he was appointed principal of the Keahua Japanese language school, Keahua, Maui, a position he held until the outbreak of World War II. An excellent writer of both tanka poems and kanshi (Chinese poems), he founded the Maui Tanka Poetry Club with Satosuke Yasui, editor of the *Maui Shimbun* (Japanese language newspaper). He was one of the most prominent leaders in Maui's Japanese community, and was especially active in youth work.

When the war broke out he was incarcerated at a temporary camp in Haiku, Maui for two months after which he was interned at the following relocation camps — Sand Island, Honolulu, Angel Island, California, Lordsburg, New Mexico, and finally Santa Fe Relocation Camp where he joined the Santa Fe-shisha Tanka Poetry Club. On December 3, 1944, he left for Crystal City, Texas to join his family who was brought over from Maui and lived there until the end of the war. During his sojourn there, he joined the Texas-shisha Tanka Poetry Club led by Dr. Mori and was instrumental in compiling the only wartime tanka anthology in the internees' camp called *Nagareboshi* (Shooting Star). In addition to this, he compiled his tanka and kanshi poems which he wrote during the war into another anthology, *Areno* (Wilderness) and published it in 1946. After the war was over, he and his family returned to Honolulu, Hawaii in December 1945.

After his return, he worked as a salesman and temporary teacher, and also as a newspaper correspondent for the *Hawaii Hochi.* Initially he joined the Choon-shisha Tanka Poetry Club, but he left in 1958 and formed a new tanka poetry club called Sankyo Tanka-sha (Valley Tanka Poetry Club) with the tanka poets who lived in Manoa Valley, Honolulu. His group published two tanka anthologies, *Yamakai I* (Valley I) and *Yamakai II* (Valley II) in 1966 and in 1972 respectively. He moved to San Francisco in 1979, but continues to edit the tanka poems written by the Sankyo Tanka-sha members for monthly publication in the *Hawaii Hochi.*

4

Sojin Takei's poems were selected from his wartime tanka anthology, *Areno,* containing 360 tanka poems published in Honolulu, August 16, 1946.

Muin Otokichi Ozaki (1904-   )

Otokichi Ozaki was born in Ikegawa-cho, Kochi-ken, Japan on November 1, 1904. After completing elementary school in Japan, Ozaki came to Hawaii at age 12 to join his parents in the remote village of Kauleau in the Chain of Craters. Soon after his arrival, he was sent to Hilo to live in the Hilo Hongwanji Betsuin Dormitory to pursue his education. After finishing junior high school and the Japanese language school, he returned to Kauleau to live with his parents, and commuted to Hilo on the train to attend Hilo High School.

In 1920, he was hired as a clerk in the management section of the *Hawaii Mainichi* (Japanese language newspaper) and three years later began his teaching career at the Hilo Dokuritsu Gakko, a job he held until December 1941. He was a very active member of the Hilo Hongwanji Buddhist Youth Club, and also participated in many social and cultural activities. In November 1923, when the first Hilo tanka poetry club, Ginushisha (Silver Rain Tanka Poetry Club) was established by two dozen of Hilo tanka poets, he was the youngest charter member at age 19. He married Hideko who also taught at the Hilo Dokuritsu Gakko and the couple had four children.

On December 7, 1941 he was arrested by the FBI and sent to the Volcano Military Camp. During the four years' internment, he was transferred from camp to camp—Sand Island, Honolulu, Angel Island, California, Fort Sill, Oklahoma, Camp Livingston, Louisiana, and Santa Fe, New Mexico. In February 1943, Ozaki was reunited with his family at Camp Jerome, Arkansas, but after two months, they were once again transferred to Tule Lake Internment Camp which was a camp for the supposedly hard core internees. There they remained until the end of the war. During his internment, he recorded his impressions and daily happenings in thousands of tanka poems. He managed to write approximately 200 poems per sheet in minute handwriting on thin ricepaper stationery which could easily be carried around without official notice.

After the war ended, he and his family returned to Honolulu in December of 1945. From 1947 to 1977 he worked at *Hawaii Times* where he eventually became the business manager. He joined the Choon-shisha Tanka Poetry Club in 1947. During this period, Ozaki helped edit two tanka anthologies, one of which was for his Hilo friend, Zanka Iwatani who had met untimely death, and the other for Soga. Zanka's tanka anthology, *Chinmoku No Toh* (Silent Tower) was published in 1954, while Soga's tanka anthology, *Keiho Kashu* was edited in 1957. In 1972, Ozaki's article on the internment was published by a prestigious literary magazine in Japan, the *Bungei Shunjyu.*

A very humble and self-effacing man, hardly anyone knew about his charity work for an orphanage in Okinawa until the Governor of Okinawa awarded him with a citation for his meritorious work. His unpretentious personality attracted many of the top people from the entertainment and literary world in Japan who eagerly sought his friendship.

Although he suffered a stroke in 1981, he has made sufficient recovery and is presently living with his wife in their Manoa home in Honolulu. At age 78, he continues to keep abreast of literary activities.

Muin Ozaki's poems were selected from the Choon-shisha tanka anthology, *Lauhala,* containing 270 tanka poems by 27 poets, published in Honolulu, January 1950.

THE EDITORS AND TRANSLATORS

Jiro Nakano, M.D. is a native of Japan and a practicing cardiologist in Hilo, Hawaii. He was Professor of Pharmacology and Associate Professor of Medicine at the University of Oklahoma College of Medicine until 1974. Presently he holds the position of Associate Clinical Professor of Medicine at the University of Hawaii John H. Burns School of Medicine. As his hobby, he writes tanka poems and English haiku, and belongs to the Ginu-shisha Tanka Poetry Club in Hilo, the Choon-shisha Tanka Poetry Club in Honolulu and the Hilo English Haiku Club. He contributes his tanka poems to the Tanka Poetry Magazine in Tokyo called *Rinkan* and his English haiku poems to *Modern Haiku* in Wisconsin and to *Cicada* in Toronto, Canada.

Kay Nakano was born and raised in Hilo, Hawaii and is the wife of Dr. Jiro Nakano. After graduating from the University of Hawaii with a major in Japanese, she received her M.S. degree in psychiatric social work in Boston, Massachusetts. She is presently a psychiatric social worker at the Hilo Counseling Center. In the last few years, she has been translating Japanese poems into English. She writes English haiku and is a member of the Hilo English Haiku Club.

Keiho Soga
Taisanboku Mori

Sojin Takei

Muin Ozaki

THE ILLUSTRATOR

George Hoshida (1907-   )

George Hoshida, born in Japan on October 23, 1907, came to Hawaii at age 5 and lived in Hilo, Hawaii until December 7, 1941. He held a job at the Hilo Electric Company for nearly 11 years. Active in community affairs, he was serving as President of the United YBA of Hilo and of the Big Island Hongwanji Judo Association at the time of the arrest. Hoshida was married, the father of three daughters with a fourth on the way, when the war broke out.

Incarcerated first at the Volcano Military Camp, Hoshida was later transferred to a series of internment camps on the mainland which included Jerome, Arkansas, Lordsburg, New Mexico, and Santa Fe, New Mexico. He was joined by his family in 1943 at Jerome Internment Camp. After the war ended, the Hoshidas returned to Hilo and

10

then moved to Los Angeles, California where they lived for 14 years. During that period, Hoshida worked as deputy clerk for the Municipal Court in Los Angeles. In 1970, Hoshida became a widower. He now lives in retirement with his second wife in Honolulu.

Hoshida's interest in art began in his early teens, and because he was unable to go to art school, he took correspondence courses in art through the American Art School and the Federal School of Art and Design. Throughout his internment, Hoshida kept a record of daily happenings in the camps through his pen and ink sketches and pastel drawings. The hundreds of sketches which were done on folder paper have been preserved in their binders as memoirs of the most unforgettable years of his life.

Arrest

torawaruru
toki wa kitarinu
ame no yoi
kokoro sadamete
kutsu no oto kiku

The time has come
For my arrest
This dark rainy night.
I calm myself and listen
To the sound of the shoes.

MP o matasete
nare ga totonoeshi
namida komorishi
kaban no omoki

While the MP's wait
You fill my suitcase
And spill your tears.
How heavy its weight.

ko no negao ni
wakarete samuku
hikare yuku
yami shojyo to
ame furi idenu

I bid farewell
To the faces of my sleeping children
As I am taken prisoner
Into the cold night rain

At The Volcano Internment Camp

yami ni narete
miwatasu naka ni
kiki nareshi
hitogoe arite
mazu ochitsukinu

I look around
The hushed darkness
In which I am settling—
I hear a familiar voice
And feel comforted, for now.

広嶋県賀茂郡川上村ニテ
布哇島ヒロ市商店主
進藤幸雨

沖縄縣國頭郡今帰仁村字古宇利二六六
布哇ヒロ市ヲラウエ街三四八九
ニテ日本語学校教師 山川武俊

KILAUEA MILITARY DETENTION CAMP.

S-25-42

shokudo ni
kayou nomi fumu
daichi nari
ajiwau gotoku
fumite ayumeri

As if to relish
Each step I take
On this great earth,
I walk —
To the mess hall.
The only walk allowed.

At The Sand Island Camp

jyuken no
saki de inu no goto
sashizu sare
munen no shinpi
muramura to tatsu

Like a dog
I am commanded
At a bayonet point.
My heart is inflamed
With burning anguish.

Keiho Soga   19

niwaka-ame ni
nokishita ni yoreba
"gerauea" to
ame no koniwa ni
oware toroburu

In the sudden downpour,
A voice whips, "Get outa here!",
As we take cover under the eaves.
Herded into a small yard,
We eat — in the rain.

ikusa hodo
kanashiki wa nashi
sekaijyu no
kanashiki koto no
koko ni atsumaru

There is nothing
More sorrowful than war.
Here alone,
All of life's sadness
Is brought together.

akatsuki no
utsuro kokoro ni
tsuma kitari
te to te o furete
yume samenikeri

As I doze at dawn,
My wife comes to me
Our hands lightly touch,
The dream is no more.

han-nen buri
tsuma to akushu shi
sono te o ba
han-nichi bakari
arawazu ni ori.

After a long half year
I take my wife's hand into mine
And for at least half a day
I do not wash away her touch.

Mama
12-20-43
8:45 P.M.
at Jerome R.C.

ori o hedate
tsuma no sumu ie
nagametsutsu
kusa no ha nado o
mushirite wa hamu

Gazing at the barracks
Where my wife exists,
Beyond the barbed wire fence,
I pluck and chew
The leaves of grass.

yume ni mishi
tsuma no omokage
yaya yatsure
kanashiki koto o
katari kerukamo

In my dream
My wife's face
Becomes drawn
As she speaks to me
Of her sorrow.

tomo wa mata
tsurezure no mama ni
hinemosu o
rakei no hito o
egaki kerukamo

My comrade,
Life-weary in the camp,
Draws pictures of nude women
All day and all night long.

On The Ship To The Mainland

isotose chikaku
suminaraitaru
kono shima no
kage kiyuru made
senso ni yoru

From the cabin window,
I bid farewell
To this fair island,
My home of fifty years,
Until its shadow disappears.

hei to narite
shita no dekki ni
ko wa noreri
chichi naru hito wa
toraware ni shite

Sailing on the same ship—
The son,
A U.S. soldier;
His father,
A prisoner of war.

Muin Ozaki   29

nobishi tsume
kamikirite futo
ko no kuse o
shikarishi koto o
omoidasareshi

Biting down my overgrown nails,
I suddenly remembered
That day
When I scolded my son
For biting his nails.

hataraku mono niwa
benjyo ni iku chansu
atauru to
kaneami goshi ni
furete yuku mono ari

"For those who work,
A chance to use the toilet"—
Brushing the wire screen
A voice calls
And disappears.

First Step On The Mainland

pokkari to
shiroki hi idenu
soko no
kiri ni tachiite
ashi no tsumetasa

I stand in the fog
Of San Francisco harbor
Where the white sun
Finally breaks open —
How cold my feet are!

aki takeno
kiri no miyako wa
yugoto ni
kanashiki omoi
hito ni semarinu

Autumn deepens
In the City of Fog.
My thoughts become heavy
With sorrows that besiege me
When evening approaches.

On The Train

meji no kagiri
tsuzuku sabaku no
hate toku
yama rokki ga
ten sosori tatsu

Far beyond the desert
As far away as the eyes can see,
Are they the Rockies
That stand erect
Against the Heavens?

ikusenri
tsuzuku areno zo
chi no hate no
yama koshi yukeba
mata areno nari

How many more thousand miles
Does this wasteland continue?
Beyond the end of the horizon
And over the mountain—
Again, more wasteland.

kisha no ushiro ni
tozakari yuku
akaki hi no
hitodama no goto
yami ni kieyuku

Behind the moving train,
A red light becomes dim
And disappears into the dark
Like the spirits of the dead.

11/9/44
3:30 PM.

M. Hiraga
Rear View

37

shoku o toru
shibashi ga hodomo
jyu mukete
kewashiki manako
hei wa sosogeru

Even for the short time
We eat our meals,
Stern and watchful gazes are cast
By soldiers standing guard
With bayonets.

Fort Sill Internment Camp

komi ageru
ikidori ari
hyakujyuichi to
munehada ni bango
akaku kakareshi

A wretching anguish rises
As the number "111"
Is painted
On my naked chest
In red.

T/5 *Shoji Fujishima*
Student Btn.— C.C.
Barrack F
Camp Savage, Minn.

1-7-44
at Jerome R.C.

Pvt. Haruto Morikawa — Age 30
Co. E 442nd Infantry #30103929
Camp Shelby, Miss.

Lordsburg I.C. North-East View from B4-Co.10-Comp.3

Lordsburg Internment Camp

takazora wa
saku naki mama ni
yugarasu
izuchi hatenami
tobitsu kieyuku

There is no fence
High up in the sky.
The evening crows
Fly up and disappear
Into the endless horizon.

yoru kudashi
ko no hisokesa wa
koya nare
tsuki samuzamu to
terasu munashisa

After nightfall
Silence envelopes
The wilderness.
The cold moon
Shines in vain.

akatsuki no
shijima yaburite
toboyuru
kayote no mure no
koe suzamajiki

How menacing the howl is,
A pack of coyotes
Breaking the silence
Of early dawn.

tsuma mo ko mo
toki sekai no
mono nariki
kono tessaku no
yoha no sabishisa

My wife and children
Live in a far away land.
How lonely are the nights
Behind these barbed wire fences.

44   Sojin Takei

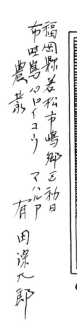

福岡縣若松市嶋郷五杣
布哇島パパイコウ　マハア
農業

有田源太郎

7-29-42

Gentaro Arita　Papaikou, Hawaii
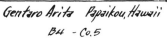
B4 - Co.5

鶴岡縣嘉穂郡祉吸村大字入水
布哇島パパイコウ　マハア
農業

安藤茂

7-29-42

Shigeru Ando　Papaikou, Hawaii
B4 - Co.5

10-12-42

45

totsu no o
sabishira ni tatsu
kakutasu ni
kataranka waga
haru no kanashimi

Should I talk
To the lonely cactus
Standing yonder in the desert
About the sorrows of Spring?

haru asaki
kimi ga chibusa no
fukurami ka
tsukitateshi mochi no
kiyoki tezawari

My hands lightly touch
The freshly pounded *mochi*
Like the swell
Of a maiden's breasts
This early spring day.

Santa Fe Internment Camp

retsu nagaku
narabu shokuji no
asa na asa na
kappu no hie no
te ni shimiru kana

I stand in line
Morning after morning,
For the cold icy cup
That pierces into my bare hands.

kogarashi ni
chiru wakuraba no
hitohira o
shizu kokoro naku
mimamorite ori

Late autumn gale —
A withered leaf flutters.
I gaze at it
With a tranquil heart.

Mr. Y. Hata - Fast Asleep.   6:45 AM 8-9-42 (Sun)

fuyu no hi ni
nagaku chi ni hiku
waga kage o
mire ba samishi mo
hosoboso to shite

My elongated shadow,
Cast on the earth
By the setting winter sun.
How lonely it looks
When reflected so thinly.

toraware no
tomo no oku wa
me ni shiruku
oini keru kamo
natsu nakaba sugu

Many a friend
Who is incarcerated
Ages visibly.
Summer is passing by.

ashi no ue ni
ari noborikuru o
jitto mitsume
toki o sugoshite
kuinu kono koro

Ants climbing up my foot —
I don't begrudge anymore
The time I spend
Just watching them.
Such is my life nowadays.

11-10-42
9:35 P.M.

Yamakawa

M. Mizutari

Ikeda

Hata

yukage ni
ukabishi hana ni
hachidori no
oto mo kasokeku
toeru shizukesa

How lonely the delicate sound
Of a hummingbird
That visits the flowers
Aglow in the beam
Of the setting sun.

Sojin Takei   55

kuchizukeru
hito shi araneba
anion no
nama o sono mama
musaborite hamu

Since there is no one
To kiss here,
I devour
One raw onion after another.

doku nomite
shiseshi tomo ari
yuyami no
kampu no michi ni
kuroki chi nagaru

A fellow prisoner
Takes his life with poison.
In the evening darkness,
Streaks of black blood
Stain the camp road.

ikameshiki
nijyu no saku no
kanata niwa
murasaki niou
yama manekiori

Beyond the forbidding fence
Of double barbed wire,
The mountain, aglow in purple,
Sends us its greetings

Tule Lake Internment Camp

"fuchusei" to
kokuin osare
Tule Lake ni
okurareshi mizo
kuyuru koto naku

"Disloyal"
With papers so stamped
I am relocated to Tule Lake.
But for myself,
A clear conscience.

An Internee Mourns
For His Son Who Died In Italy

rosoku ni
hi tomosu kimi ga
oishi te no
hosori yori noboru
kemuri hitosuji

As Thou light a candle
A thin thread of smoke
Rises ever so faintly
Between Thine aged hands.

Death At The Camp

suna kuruu
areno ni toha ni
nemuritaru
tomo no sabishisa
omoi namidasu

The barren wasteland
Raged by sand storm,
I weep for my friend
Who sleeps there alone,
Eternally.

Entrance to Gila R.C. Butte camp 4/19/44 East View Canal camp in the distance

11/19/44
Gila R.C.
South View
Butte p.

gojuyo no
torawarebito ga
yoritsudoi
iwashi no akikan de
shoko o suru

Fifty and more
Of us prisoners gather here
To burn incense
On an empty sardine can
For the repose of a departed soul.

warera mina
sarinishi ato no
kono mushiro
tare ka touran
ikusa hate naba

When the war is over
And after we are gone
Who will visit
This lonely grave in the wild
Where my friend lies buried?

ikumannen
kusa nomi oishi
kono areno
aware hakanaki
hone mittsu umu

In this desolate field
Where only weeds have grown
For millions of years,
We mournfully bury
Three comrades
Who died in vain.

junjitsu no
uchi ni ryoyu
mitari yukinu
kono tatakai no
hate o mizushite

Within just ten days
Three fellow internees
Depart from this world
Never to see
The end of this war.

Homecoming

akibae no
yaseshi ga hitotsu
tobimawaru
nibuki yuhi no
heya no akarumi

A thin autumn fly
Circling the room
Lit by a dim evening sunlight.

Sojin Takei   67

ikuman o
kazofuru kuroki
tori no mure
kemuri o nashite
doyomi tobitatsu

A flock of black birds
Ten thousand in number
Creates a commotion
As they fly up like smoke.

asahikage
kagami no gotoku
terikaesu
imashi watarinu
kororado no kawa

With morning sunlight
Reflecting,
We now cross
The Colorado River.

yonen mae o
kataru funaji no
nadarakasa
utsushi yo wa geni
yume no mata yume

Sailing the same sea —
How smooth this voyage is
After four long years.
The present world
Is a dream within a dream.

aoumi no
aosa ni somite
tobiuo wa
namima o nuite
aobikari suru

Stained in blue
By the blue ocean,
The flying fish
Fly between waves,
Shining blue.

島根縣邇摩郡久利村大字今市大〇八〇
ハワイ、ホノルル市モイリリ西本願寺
開教使
薮谷晃道
五十五歳

橫井縣舟生郡立待村杉
道生寺
似従オアフ、ワイアルア、本願寺
開教使
柏　龍天
五十歳

北海道北見古野村〇〇
Pasadena Cal:
杉町八重光（四三）

嶋根縣簸川郡西濱村
三原源治（三二）
SEATTLE, WASH.

広島縣比婆郡敷信村
ビス食堂
Honolulu
重永茂夫

愛媛縣溫泉郡睦野村
片本〇郎
Honolulu Hawaii

Koko Head
Diamond mo
mejika nari
asahi kagayou
umi no akarusa

Koko Head nears,
And now Diamond Head!
How bright the sea is
Shining in morning sunlight!